wrim
Paige Menton

SPUYTEN DUYVIL

New York City

ISBN 978-1-959556-17-6

Library of Congress Cataloging-in-Publication Data

Names: Menton, Paige, author.
Title: Wrim / Paige Menton.
Description: New York : Spuyten Duyvil, 2023.
Identifiers: LCCN 2023000431 | ISBN 9781959556176 (paperback)
Subjects: LCGFT: Poetry.
Classification: LCC PS3613.E4965 W75 2023 | DDC 811/.6--dc23/eng/20230206
LC record available at https://lccn.loc.gov/2023000431

CONTENTS

Up until

in the middle the middle of

what will hover
    on this day   and

allow me to hear

                                  misplaced

          labors to know wealth
                                 somewhere
             a morning arrival of birds
    in search of a story

        we will plant

           handshakes

passports   photographs and

wisps of hair   plant grocery lists and permission slips

            what is the word for the part of each leaf that
connects its stem to the branch the part that gives in
           the abscission zone
             the bottom layer expands in the fall and
breaks the weak walls of the top layer and this is happening presently all
around me one leaf at a time resigned by wind or force of rain or magical
realism

                                        how our maps lead us

                                   valences of cryptic
                                        insulation for
                                   stories running throughout

                                        our collective
learning

                                        how
we recognize the bluebirds   by the playful way
they dart in circles from tree to ground

all these ounces of

experience

and the views from the window and the briefest glimpses backwards

across a lifetime as rare as blackberry cobbler

how many abscission zones ruptured right in front of me today how
many sandhill cranes undetected overhead

I
think like spokes in a wheel

when the grains obscure, seek the pattern

the upper or outer edge of an object, typically something circular
or approximately circular, as in a china egg cup with a gold rim or
the verb to form or act as an outer edge or rim for, as in a huge lake
rimmed by glaciers

      or a limit or boundary as in the outer rim of the solar system
or an encircling stain or deposit such as a thick rim of suds from the
Old English rima meaning a border or coast

                                            fringe, frame,
margin, hem, periphery, skirt, verge, brink, crest, curb, cusp, lip,
boundary, brim, compass, confines, circumference and Old English
saerima for seashore or rim of the sea when you cross out the extrane-
ous and are left at the edge when you have lived thus far and sit at the
edge or cusp or brim and fail to see over the edge imagine a precipice
or a valley or simply continuing down the road when the steps feel like
a continuation but clouds obscure the view ahead when the all clear
may or may not pertain

                                      when only the words connect you
with the rim of the sea when you are not ready to see a limit or bound-
ary but you feel you are exiting one all the same

minutes passed along an axis bent

even at the defining line there is

capillary action

like the paper folded in half

suggests desperation and a physical force unnamed that implies a leap

bend ideas like

a funnel toward a center that contains seeds

pat some soil on top and water

a kind of patience like ink

collating whispers and inhalations

that shine toward the rim of

exactly   which resonance

think about tomorrow as a barrel or pulpit or container ship

like ribbon unfurling

that project of eternal   locomotion

always
trodden within
the same concentric paths through little bluestem past shagbark hickory past a
knob kneed bald cypress past the row of utility towers past the ponds fading to
be reclaimed

we depart
knowing full well our inadequacy

to cover the hole

cut in ways uncharted like a dull knife

we rest
at this edge of reverse or full speed ahead from lightning bugs to lights out
my extirpated generation   the junco returned
today with a flock of chipping sparrows
   the junco returned last year with a flock of chipping sparrows

     hidden in houses all over the world are lists like mine made by
people like me who
need to record when the indicator species leave and return who need to
document the patterns
     to know our Goliath feet have not crushed the
breath out of every living thing just yet   sheet metal
    swizzle stick   bubble
wrap
     cat litter
            sit and spins
          wonder twins
       we are not at the edge of our knowledge

facing each horizon bravely and with proper posture

the hint

slides away

crusty and equipped   like a

tightrope walker

we

remain silent between   gloss   and   precision

as

the circus performer

and

push to the edge to balance the awakened against the brambles or

nightshade

how you interpret

the outline

is compressed   in

margins

from generation to

generation until the need no longer presents itself

in any future plans

the crepuscular

circling of two bats in summer

    must be included I woke up thinking of transcendence and I
come from Alabama and want to go home

    here
a mockingbird just perched outside my window and that is rare enough to
record

                we are all just collections of future
artifacts

    we brace for the winds and count the meadows
when the intention is to pour we still resist opening all the valves

                the ditherings
            obscured by static

and tidy tiny movements

rather a curation

the first-person singular as a step

                                                    toward

the future
                                    that zeal and
                                    singular
focus
                    like
        an exhalation

of

syllables which

repeat syllables

all alertness

yet constricting

I

claim

                a
house full of lifetime   an assemblage
of antler and skull acorns and mica flakes quartz and fossils left in red rock
catalpa pod spilling over onto the floor its feathery seeds

polymath lab

once upon a time I learned

bustle

always more than one iron in the

sunset

like a hundred pages

in the streams and the feeds in

the fire that hangs over us

the potential

smooth

sound   of

strength

in the center
we are
both and all because we can

search any   point

on the globe right over the edge

as the horizon diminishes

                            perhaps
when you are not   threatening to

                             tell me all the ways in which I
                                      resist
     the story underneath
                          I

                          will

       write an homage to
           the first person
                  who kept asking questions and

       wondered what they discussed
in
           the tops of trees with their warnings and
interruptions
                            grass stems
blowing their yellow to brown range of suggestion

Edge Object 1

Crater Lake is deep water in a sleeping volcano

                        the
deepest lake in this country and

        often obscured by clouds

                                considered too sacred to
view

                        the purity of its color   how far down one
can sink from the edge and the inherent danger of that sinking the vio-
lence of its creation and potential future eruption volcanoes abstract like
dinosaurs often in the same chapter yet a breathing presence in this story
the fire below the cataclysm contrasted with such serenity to
still   mix with all the edges that bind
        mix with a
map to every future destination   with the geology of relationship
with fair distribution of wealth and labor mix with the unpaid time that
fails to fill the gas tank   with the brimming over and the
caldera of any given moment
with the fire that hangs over and its burning of the roads its acidification
of the waters
                                                mix with the
scratch off national parks poster   that appeared
on my phone yesterday so tangible and collectible as if the deepest lake
could be poured in my purse

floating along and unyielding

Erosion haunts
because of what it takes or because of what it leaves behind?

The potential always there to fill in gaps with what we expect to see how fragile the rim of our order and orders, and

also, how resistant

Make our unknown known and keep the unknown always just beyond

enclosed and muted yet flowing within a tight periphery

It is
assumed that I can be interrupted. For minutes or months or decades. I as-
sume this as do others around me. At the level of sentence or hour or thought
or plan. The extent to which I am complicit in this and the reasons why and
the resolutions. Here and now

I am complicit as
the centuries as the way it has always been as the best survival rates as the
need to nurture as the caregiver as all of that.

roar should be the response at the rim, forcing at least an echo

for as long as I can remember feverish in the
feeling that time is rushing past

since I was three and refused to take naps,
frightened of missing daytime

How to inhabit the circles and the curved lines

This word humble could attach to that word spider that could adjoin
another small animal such as vole and populate a paragraph with willow
leaves or tourniquets or moonlight.

Notice the elusive subject, the hole at the center, perhaps the missing link or merely the voice of the moment to speak of the holy and the diminished.

About many untold pairs of words whittled into nebulous

1

Is the life additive or a scraping away? Are the solutions a pile of pillows or a net unwoven and restrung? The story is always the beginning, the middle, and the end, what remains at its periphery and the hollowed out and the fat. The story begs to be told, demands to be shelved, whispers, pivots, blushes, shines, and cowers. It blends fact with machismo or charisma or recipes or mistaken folklore. The story is rusty, leans on the hood of the car, begins in Nashville or Tulsa or along the Natchez Trace. The story contains alligators and guitar picks, nothing that is not familiar. It contains sleights of hand delivered in calm and quiet to a spellbound audience of three. The story resists its retelling, denies itself, refuses to answer further questions, counters its narrative with a practiced deflection. The story wears pearls and never drinks. When encountering any personality survey, the story adopts an answering strategy similar to working out a quilt pattern or list of knitting directions. If it were called for jury duty, it would be eliminated due to its opposition to the death penalty. It contains multitudes but resists flood insurance. Which side will you take in the story? Have you heard this story before? The story develops like a scaffold like a manicure like a quick jaunt into an old-fashioned phone booth, the clear kind with the bell painted on top in blue. I would like to test the memory of the story, to ask it a few questions about that night, about that incident, but I do not want to frighten or cause undue stress.

Does the story wish for a glass of water, a comfortable chair, some paper and a pencil, some time to think? We will just step out for a moment to allow it to collect its thoughts, to catch its breath. Is the story testing the climate, feeling the pulse of the moment, as it were, resisting simple answers to difficult questions, investing its best thinking into our collective future? Without writing us off, is the story reading more like an open book? Is the story yearning for a greater understanding, an appreciation of new indicators, new variables? How does the story prove itself? How does the story choose its own adventure? To whom does the story look for solace? Does it have a shoulder to cry on? Would we share the shoulder if we share the story? Does each story need such a shoulder? The story ceases these questions, intuits answers according to season and mood, according to the angle of light through the curtains. It remains a little bashful in social situations, likes to look at its shoelaces, examines the vein patterns of leaves closely unbidden. That we all might know such a story. That it might come visit, might grace the halls of higher learning, might open a window for us into its creative process, signal its intent to discover new things, might shed light on future solutions to so many things. We check it for any signs, and all the stories which follow it. We are always on the lookout for such stories, the ones that leave us on the edge of our seats, that force us to look within, to come up wanting. We hope that we might write such a story. We hope that we may be such a story. Some of us are. Some of us write around the edges, type in steady spirals toward a certain center, like the Fibonacci flow of sunflower seeds encircled by browning petals. There is the story and the scene before. The scene after could contain a dialogue or a river, chestnuts for sale from a street vendor, crisp air, snowflakes in late December. The scene after would need to change location. Time flows in all directions some say, including perhaps the writer of this story.

      The trick of the story is to get at the root, the words sequestered just over the rim, just against the walls, below the pebbles falling now, below the changing weather. The story at the root frightens really, and for this, it remains in the center, which is dark and deep. There are no figures here. There are only hiding places, some moisture for lack of sun, a hint of bioluminescence. Can the story hear the waterfall, understand the paintings on the rock faces, arrange the leaves at the surface in a pleasing circle reminiscent of the rim, recollecting the deciduous forests full of ash and elm before the story? The scene before the story includes polar bears because such scenes often do. The journalists remark on the appearance of polar bears in every one of the scenes before the story. The children have listened to the scene before the story, have not lived through the scene, and will not live in a scene ever like that scene after or during the story. We all dance around the story, and we remain now in the story. We may speak or scream or stand in rows waiting or revolve in and out of buildings through glass. There are no appropriate expressions. The setting contains some green, some blue. Of most things we are certain.

2

The seasons reach into us.
The narrative includes much speculation, allows for an insistent manipulation
of fact. They publish it anyway. Part of the center involves a naming of sub-
jects, an accounting of players and pawns, kingdoms, phyla, classes, orders,
families. What is the plot within this plot? Crack that open and win a prize. To
be an imaginist trapped inside a glass box as the sun sets. Not trapped really
because words open doors, as they say.

Grey squirrels will be needed to
populate the future story, when other populations have seen reductions. The
squirrel visible at dusk will greet us with the dawn.

Draw an undulation into existence and pray. See the faith in the curves, the mathematics in the shadow of afterthought.

Dandelion, muscadine, clover, white pine, carpet of zoysia, Southern magnolia, crepe myrtle, and landscaping of river rock. The literal accompaniments are rarely flashy or distinguished. A coating or insulation, a band of mental reinforcement, path of most resilience. Rarely tinged with poverty, mostly outward facing, searching for astronomy while looking down for arrowheads.

3

We migrate like the birds that
hesitate in their breeding grounds to eat a heavy mast of nuts and
fruits. We migrate like butterflies and seek safety for our young. We
are rarely reckless when we defend our children.

We can always plan. These plans manifest as education or investment or hoarding or patience. We can repurpose any byproducts, scan the horizon for outliers, line our doubts with newspapers and dried leaves. The horizon of others may be fully vested. Most likely. We can carry scorn like a rash on the back of our hands. Time to humidify and adorn with tiny white lights. Time to bake bread. Restore senses with a faith in the yeast rising, with the years crisping at the edges, ripening. The sun today will carry a promise which sounds like a myth which sounds like a self-help manual which sounds like a prayer. We draw ourselves to the sun as we do to the moon because we see the circles of our eyes. We see the circles as the bicycle wheels of the bike we sold so many years ago. We buy and sell in the cycles of days, and we do other things. We light candles and relish the circle of light around the wick. Once we made candles by rolling beeswax sheets of red, gold, blue, and green. We gave these as gifts, as we gave other handmade gifts which were saved or discarded. We relish the lessons and proximity. At any angle we reckon with a slew of tiny choices, with leaves strewn and collected. There could be an inventory of verbs and adverbs. The nouns are not fixed. Many were fashioned as instruction, but they can also be folded, piled into a drawer or storage shed. The nouns may be captured in photographs. A very few nouns run in the blood, remain undetected or suspicious, wait like spores for the spring rains. These nouns may prove guttural or obstinate like sleeper cells. We will just have to wait and see. As we wait to know the empathy of the sun.

4

One story contained the harried mother
who wanted a ride in the country anywhere. That
story contained dilapidation at home and on the road, inching past
soot-covered houses that mourned their time and season.
That story included

much less

experience with the conceptual geography, less history and mileage.
How much of life is
giving the stories the wrong titles, slotting them into false genres.

Like breath, like breeze, like new sun on diminished ground, we iso-
late, consider, search the sky

for migrants, search the ground for smooth stones. Of this entire text
to be a magic 8 ball. Blacken the water and shake.

Include stout oak trees and a shag-
bark hickory at least two hundred years old.

The story
revisits similar scenes, adds texture in the form of newly fallen oak
leaves or a trio of active squirrels. The story absorbs and rarely yields.
When sponge is the steady state, where does the flow appear?

ruptures occur in everyday practices

Six pheasants cross the road to get to the field of corn. They astonish and we are still, taking in their vibrant reds and blue-greens while we calculate the rarity they represent near our house where once they were common. Ring-necked and skittish, they may enter our view simply because they were presented to the land, stocked for hunters to find.

      More common to us now is the bird we find later perched above a lake: bald eagle, majestic comeback kid all smug up high, surveying. The story today took to the road to take in a system. The story today included walks without words, the sudden disturbances of oak leaves, some soup and a sandwich, and a radio that failed to find a station anywhere. Drive down a new street to find your face in the windows, shuttered churches and converted churches. Church on a hill with a roof that will never leak. Take in the signs celebrating the president, the more numerous banners celebrating the high school football team, and imagine a life of such generational unity.

      Gateway to anthracite, subtext of all the stories behind the curtains, nailed beneath the new siding, embedded in the sidewalks.

      Enter the town a dozen times and see nothing. Start to scratch the surface after you interview a thousand people or live there twenty years, but you won't do either of those things, just think about the surface and its inevitability as you pass through.

Stood beside a meander today.

One person who visits that creek carves his initials in a bridge every December, for the last sixteen years at least. What has he noticed? What have the rangers noticed about him?

The story of an almost anonymous ritual.

Step lightly.

Stories of others of once common pheasants crossing the road right and left to get to the fields of corn. Stories of the common bluebirds, the common foxes, the common bobcats, the common phoebes and buntings, the common orchids and spring beauties, the common ramps and paw paw. Stories of common lakes iced over.

the grains

Nothing fills

the words

waiting to be pushed.

my

stubborn   way

each syllable into its self-sustaining particles

                                                    One story is

the need
to

                    retrace

                    traveled spaces that held
light

ghost of a circle   Tangents can crust the edge, cushion
the leap, insulate the voice crying into the echo chamber.

draw a line
straight through the circle, which can be done an infinite number of times,
directing you to two distinct points each time.
Are the two points digressions?

                    Or simply a pretty picture.

            to   erode

        defined   the

course   from
behaving   like

water   or

        distant   movements

            the story   collected
                on   a trail
            crisscrossing
                            patience

You may teeter.

Do we need dragons
and sea monsters and giant bears or   silence?

          This is all conjecture, and the air is cold.

to contain all the geographies

We know that each step contains within it
the location of every step we have taken before: down the grocery store
aisles, into cathedral pews, across narrow mountain streams, into jail
cells, up the hills of a neglected cemetery, down the ladder into a hidden
cave, out into still river water to wash hair. Make our tracks bioluminescent

follow each glow-in-the-dark
path at its ground level while viewing it from above, its wide canvas and
web. The filaments stretch across the rim, capture a hold from edge to
edge, represent the risk of the spider spinning its way across. Spin

enough filament to make a net. Erase then the rim. Bounce.

The fibers of kudzu vine of wool of
hair of reed of spent daylily leaves. Return to weaving a fiber history, return to the wife of the architect in the modern wood house in the woods
with a giant loom. She wove on that loom, and you do not recall if she
considered herself an artist. You do not recall if she was weaving while
you visited with your parents and discussed plans for a house that was
never built. You do not really understand why you were there, and you
vaguely recall that the architect and his weaving wife had a few children,
perhaps all daughters, and you remember light in the house and some
items and furniture in casual, productive disarray.

You wonder what your mother
remembers of this exchange or visit, her point of view so contained in
her adulthood and long- ago mission filled with hope and continuity.
A world away. We all have those worlds away. This sticks in your world

away because it demonstrated a pair of creative beings in a space they fashioned for themselves in the woods, out of the main. And a woman's tool for art took up an entire room, or at least the better part, as your five or six-year-old eyes took it in. These people were probably young then as your parents were young then, parents of young children who needed a home built by this architect. Your father was squandering the money to build this home, and that is another story. Part of the world away, the Venn diagram of worlds inhabited by your father and you and your mother and others.

the glistening and the apprehension, the fretting

Spilling over an edge is waterfall.

                                        Once you
stood under a waterfall and gazed through the cascade, or did you just
watch another person do this, afraid of the force? Once you found an
arrowhead, after a childhood of searching,
turned your eyes to the flint at your feet at the right second. Near the
waterfall under which you may or may not have stood.

          a waterfall is incontrovertible and, therefore, perhaps catching.
To be so sure. So confident in one's response to the edge, so inevitable
and without great strain

Almost a clear point A to point B. Punctuation of geologic sentences,
exclamation of the unseen forces, the plates at play, and the glacial hol-
lowing out of the down below.

that visit
one end of
our sake
how
herculean
with
out
state
again
asking and
failing to
return

Edge Object 2

       Walk over the line, not the finish line, not the receding line, not the line of demarcation or the Maginot line or the Mason-Dixon line or the international date line. Not the line of remembering and forgetting, perhaps more akin to the looking glass or the wardrobe, and from the children should we learn. We have walked the line, but we have to step over now, or push it back, or smudge it out. We have been fed a line, but we can no longer bite. No more tricks with lures, no more bait.

Obscured by the tree line, the dead ash.

Skirt around

the track once laid.

Even as these words   land in

threads

The home fiber.

The track record is a seepage

a soundtrack, a trace.

the counter to the echo

Philippe Petit sliced the air between the Twin Towers, built a vocabulary from void. His words did not come with permission, but he was lauded nonetheless. How to build more words from that affrontery. High-wire words cut with timing and precision. They empty and push just beyond the dust left behind.
They include few conditionals but
all the tenses. They stretch or shrink to fit the specific edge considered.

Single birds lift from the ground and from tree branches behind this window and volley forward across a wide space and into cover, from one edge of protection to another, like words spoken.

Any
event can contain bold words, which may indicate the health of the participants or a need to shape conduct.

You can hide the boldness behind the potted plants and new light fixtures. An aureole of brilliant green and yellow light, transfixing. We might walk past the bluebirds on a different occasion, unaware that like the cedar waxwings, they blend noiselessly into the russet leaves of the oak. Skitter and skate across the nearby air currents, eager to live. Our relationship to gravity is rarely tested and usually not especially adventurous.

Talking in

so many concentric circles fading into the gaze of the bald eagle perched on that branch up there. The bald eagle does not share the story and is spared the angst.

Our experience of encountering him on that branch will live on in us, but our appearance in his life will not, has not, registered in his. His future carried in our past. We will purchase car chargers, pay local and federal taxes, signal when turning right, donate cans to food banks, and remember him. Any person, regardless of political party, would stare in awe at a bald eagle perched nearby.

We like to talk about looking for common ground. What is the story in that? Where does it live: in the ground, above the ground, under the ground, in a treasure chest locked for the next hundred years, as a grand prize in a game show, in a vault just north of the North Sea?

What again, in this day and age, as they say, was the story? Who wants to share?

The steady

                              steady

                    stiff

                          civic

             hum

           reminds

                 Many of us

            to

     scarcely

             imagine the world

                 Some of us

venture

like constellations, like spreadsheets

to account for the length of a sigh, the decibels
associated with sunflowers turning, the number of bluebirds that pass by the
homes we have mounted for them.

The Ring of Fire is an anticipating, pulsating dragon.

                                  this constant silent smolder

                     mitigating

                                      its revenge

At this moment, in this seemingly calm location, a grey squirrel, one of nearly a dozen bisecting the front yard this morning, desperately wants the window to dissolve. He hops and grabs the glass, retreats, tries again, as if he can will it away. What appears more promising in here than the mast of red oak acorns right out there? How do the other squirrels, who have never sustained such an interest in this interior, communicate futility to him? Or do they? Is he merely asking a question they have never considered and therefore could not know the answer? Is he a grey squirrel innovator? Is he exhibiting a behavior that will aid in squirrel evolution or mark him for a premature death?

Grey squirrels are your constants, and you do not know the constants of Hawaii or Japan or Kiribati, where the people speak English or Gilbertese. A language named for a British captain. The bokikokiko, a bird, is the only endemic land species on Kiribati. Many of the indigenous species have become extinct due to human disruption, including phosphate mining. One chain of tiny islands: 32 atolls and one raised coral island, actually. A frigate bird is featured on the Kiribati flag. The president of Kiribati has already purchased land on Fiji to move his people there before the inevitable diminishment of his country into the Pacific Ocean. Will the frigate bird fly into the Fiji flag? Fiji is composed of islands too. Why are they more resilient than Kiribati, more tenable in the long term? How long is the long term? Each of these cultures can fill books and books and has. Each squirrel is a book, each frigate bird. Each Polynesian rat, now present in Kiribati, introduced. The space heater has been on briefly. It figures sporadically in this narrative because it is here and consumes energy, which connects it to the bokikokiko which connects it to the grey squirrel. Squirrels also make guest appearances throughout this narrative because they are observable elements of the story,

part of the main. How many bokikokiko survive, and will they be trans-
ferred to Fiji when the people of Kiribati depart their home? What are
the consequences either way? Is anyone considering them? How many
individuals not living on Kiribati have travelled there simply to see the
bokikokiko? How often does a resident of Kiribati see one? Are they
like the blue jay of Kiribati? And what about all the endemic species in
all the flood-prone, about-to-be deluged parts of the world? What is the
plan for them as the people flee to higher ground? Who is working on
this? You turn the space heater off. Back to Noah and the ark. Arks of en-
demic species, each containing the species accustomed to living together
in their own remote location, each circumnavigating the globe forever.

A public hanging and the eight-year-old who saw it. Thirty-eight
Sioux prisoners killed by the United States government in the larg-
est mass hanging in American history. December 26, 1862, and your
great-great-grandfather was there in Mankato, Minnesota.

How to contain a humanity within. How to breathe such light air, such
lightness. These are the days and these others. Hold your feet to the ring
of fire.

your father never told a single story about growing up

He did not demonstrate reluctance, just extended absence until it was permanent.

The building blocks of the story, the proto-story, gap-toothed, chipped.

If

he had known that he needed to hurry.

It is cavernous what you don't know.

Through and

1

The story contains a self-made character who studies hard, advances beyond her social class, blends in with the learned, and disappears. The story wonders why this person wishes to stand in the background, why this person remains so quiet. Is the person too meek to succeed? Prone to melancholy? Storing up her potential to spring open in grand exhibition? Is the person secretly writing another story of success, perhaps with a different publisher who does not traffic in words? What is this person afraid of exactly? The story does not know, does not have access to the inside track, and must wait in suspense like the rest of us. The story is peppered with questions and remains mute, attentive, slightly vexed, and impatient. The story is not aware of any natural impediments to the main character arriving at her purpose. The story has not made any secret deals or contracts or proprietary agreements with other potentially more focused, more inspiring and fantastic main characters. The story watches the oak leaves fall just like everybody else and waits, occasionally checking text and emails, resenting the presence of leaf blowers in modern American society and the preponderant noise they pump into the surrounding air. The story agrees that there are some holes in the narrative arc, but the story can be patient. The story can listen, empathize, nod at the right moments, feign agreement when necessary. The story has attended some useful workshops and could point the main character to some helpful titles and videos. In fact, the story knows of an excellent retreat center if the main character is interested. The story wishes the main character would speak to more people about her concerns and above all, learn to network. The story is sensitive to offering unsolicited advice to the main character, likes to honor the golden rule. The story has not yet encouraged other characters to prod the main character toward self-inquiry but may explore this route if the main character continues to stagnate like water in a detention basin. The story prefers more elegant similes and is inclined to include dialogue and photos with clever captions. The story prefers to work while listening to movie soundtracks from the eighties, a trait shared with the main character, although the main character has not engaged in this behavior in several years since digital technology and its attendant devices revolutionized the ways in which people gather, store, and play their favorite music. The main characters' favorite cassettes, for example, are nearby but no longer accessible, and she has failed to make a steady acquaintance with online platforms. She feels that her resistance to this shows her age, and therefore she resists demonstrating this resistance and just ignores the whole thing altogether, leaving her world deprived of background music and the possible inspiration such music could provide. She intends to correct this one day, just as she tells the story that she plans to clean out her closets, determine a retirement funding scheme, and track a path toward her ultimate purpose. The story nods encouragingly again and asks gently how to be helpful.

The main character is too steadfast in her attachment to the periphery. She will just think about this tomorrow, makes a note to contemplate the growing power and influence of the story tomorrow after she gets a haircut, turns in the library books, and buys eggs and coffee. After she weeds, does the laundry, puts away the breakfast dishes. The main character carries most of these tasks in her head as a refrain and does not feel the need to write them on a list., tries to use the list for more important tasks. The main character plans to think deeply after lunch. She has read that it is most useful to block out time in your day to think deeply, and she intends to do this after she takes her son to the doctor appointment. The main character has read that the main characters of other stories achieve their star status as the most celebrated main characters in their fields by routinely blocking off these times to think deeply and develop big ideas.

                                                            She knows, however, that the story is a quick study. The story may appear to be gazing at squirrels or contemplating embroidery patterns, but the story has to eat too, you know. The story is cold, and the main character is cold, and they discuss the wasted energy of space heaters before deciding that they would turn one on for just a little bit. The main character is deeply, almost despondently concerned about the future of the climate and the planet's biodiversity. The story has read the news reports and tries to comfort the main character. The story is also concerned about the climate in an existential threat what-can-one-little-person-do-about-it kind of way. The story mirrors the opinions of many politicians who together represent more than one little person and could in fact do quite a lot about it, could corporately change the fate of the planet. The story thinks about this dilemma while the space heater drowns out any outside noises. The main character takes in the rattle of the main heating system and the steady roar of the space heater and considers revolution, or at least a call-in campaign, and remembers that she has a responsibility to urge citizens to call their member of Congress, a particular member of the House of Representatives, who once made a promise and now needs to keep it to tip the balance and sow the seeds of bipartisan agreement in these troubled times.

The main character listened earlier in the day to some lectures about British literature in the nineteenth century and now wishes to read and perhaps teach *Oliver Twist* and *Wuthering Heights* and *Jane Eyre*. The main character knows that she cannot assign all of these texts, but she finds literature to be endlessly deep and rich in providing examples of how to live our best lives. She likes the idea of understanding what Dickens aimed to do with his novels—change the social order-- and she would like to experience firsthand the genius of Emily Brontë in the debut and only novel that she completed in her too brief life. The main character would like to be the principal in her own narrative, but she is not much interested in penning narratives as they arise out of her own mind. The story would like the main character to settle on what she most wants to do and then simply set about doing that thing and letting the story carry on. The story wonders if it will ever be strong enough to change the social order. The story is not aware of too many stories that have succeeded with that task. The story needs to take a walk and think about literal and figurative next steps. The main character tends to wallow in the figurative, and the story wants to prod the main character forward. The main character wants to keep her job, after all, with regard to the story and agrees to meet the next day for coffee. The story gives the main character some notes about the social order, kind of like homework, for the main character to review that evening. The main character is extremely interested in disrupting the social order but does not know where to begin. The main character falls asleep that night murmuring the words to "Let There be Peace on Earth."

The main character awakens with a new resolve, full of that expansive sense of possibility and faith in her own ingenuity and grit. The main character is savvy, after all, and knows savvy people. The main character is prepared to face the story with more specifics and more action items, more concrete and measurable objectives, something she should have learned about in graduate school but has pieced together since then. The main character wishes to set all self-help jargon aside, or at least to stop reading it, and she denies herself some cereal for breakfast. She sees this small step as emblematic of striving for a higher ideal, an indication of developing the much-needed habit of deep thought. After she develops this habit and the pattern of setting aside sufficient time, she will not need breakfast cereal. The main character will not run marathons, but she will naturally engage in some high-performing hobbies like climbing mountains. The main character will not continue to build insufferable mountain metaphor on top of insufferable mountain metaphor, however, but may employ photos of actual visited and perhaps summited mountains in future public relations. The main character dresses for her coffee date with the story, choosing her favorite socks and boldest sweater. It would be effective for the main character to book some time with deep thought before this meeting, but she needs to make a grocery list and water all the houseplants. The main character might think deeply on the ride to the coffee shop, or she might listen to "Wait, Wait, Don't Tell Me."

The story is already seated at a small round marble top table with a mocha in a mug and the *Book Review*. The story glances up and greets the main character casually. The story mentions a flattering review of the current poet laureate's latest book. Retreat center webpages flash before the main character's eyes as she hangs her coat on her chair. The story thinks back to the interior monologue of questions from the day before, and the story sips. The main character meets the story's gaze and reveals her first thoughts of the morning, her ideas for research and writing projects to pursue. The story waits. The story is not that devil on one shoulder, angel on the other. The story is not a Debbie downer. The story is the living vessel for the main character to pour all that potential into, not quite an alter ego or a shadow. Is the story a Tinker Bell to the main character's Peter Pan? Hard to tell. Over the years, the story has lost sight of the story's relationship to the main character, but the story continues to progress, nonetheless. Perhaps it is this progression that the main character most fears, that the story will move beyond her control, that the story will tell itself and leave her behind. That she will not be the shaper of the story but the shaped. That the story will take off or fade away, refuse to take her calls, settle on another main character even. She should explain this to the story. She should lay it all out, to the story and to herself. She knows that this is the hardest part, figuring out what the it is to lay out. She is right at the point of understanding something important, and she wants to run. She maintains her steady gaze and upper body control as she sits down. The main character takes the first section of the paper, opens it, and raises it up to appear to be reading. The story does not seem to mind this because a review of a biography is quite engrossing. The main character thinks. What must she lay all out? The fear of being left behind. The greater fear of already having been left behind and how to recover lost ground. The fear that the plot is pointless. The fear that the plot lacks greater purpose. The fear that the plot wastes more time and talent. The fear that meandering has not been good enough, that meandering is a desired but ultimately fruitless approach to the plot, that meandering is not a recognized plot-development method, that recognized methods outweigh and outlast preferred methods. The fear that other characters are and will remain discouraging. The fear that other characters who have not yet been will become discouraging. The fear that her preferred meandering will endanger the future livelihood of some other characters. The fear that the main character's hopes and dreams simply will not pan out. The fear of poverty in the future. That last one is a big fear, and the main character careens wildly in her mind from the aspirational to the practical from one moment to the next, or at least to received notions of what it means to be practical, and this raises her fears because of the extent to which she has failed to be practical up to this point in the story. The story knows about some of these fears. The story has an intuitive sense about some of these fears, without the fears being spelled out. The main character wants to come clean and itemize all of these concerns, if only to be reassured that all will be well, that poverty is not on the horizon. The main character already senses some resentment from the other characters for taking the time to write out these notes to better inform the story of her thinking. These notes are the closest that the main character has come to deep thought in some time.

2

The story remains expectant. The story could be about so many other things, after all, and the story is always in search of compelling characters. The main character certainly tries the patience of the story, but they do go way back. The story met the main character when they were kids, elementary school, in fact. The main character started by writing about witches using vacuum cleaners instead of brooms. The story was impressed. The main character created an interview between Jane Pauley and a Martian and over the years wrote many poems and a short story about a boy confined by his mother to a single white room. The main character decided to focus on the poems once she went to college, and the story kept in touch, continued to encourage. The main character did not feel that writing poems served the greatest social good when she left college, so she went to graduate school to be a teacher, and the story followed her, curious about this decision and its effect on the poetry writing. The main character did not perceive that others might consider the poetry writing a hobby now. She did not think about it that way, but she found it difficult to have more than one focus, and she had so much time, after all. So much time. One thing and then another. Upon reflection, the main character is now a little baffled that the story has stuck around so long. What could impress the story now? Might the story really be itching for a new collaborator, someone with more pizzazz? The main character has enjoyed most of the plot elements up to this point, even as they have pattered along quietly, humbly, without much monetary compensation and little societal respectability. The main character does not face open hostility or disrespect. The main character has never been shamed or mistreated or violated or endangered. The main character has much to be grateful for. With her previous accolades and early promise, however, she does not seem to be reaching her maximum potential in our achievement culture. The story has held on because of the potential and early promise. The story still remains curious. The story has given some thought to the merits and negative implications of the achievement culture, perhaps not the deep thought required, but some consideration. The story believes in the late bloomer, or in this case, the early bloomer hibernating to emerge as a late bloomer. The story feels that the main character has a right to change plots and may not have had a full sense of where to take the story when she was younger and accepted so many received ideas. The story senses that the main character has arrived at an edge now, a point of departure toward a greater and more directed focus, and the main character just needs to determine the area of focus. As if. With all this backstory, one might lose sight of the pending conversation for which the main character has just arrived and seated herself. The story looks up from the book review and asks the main character to describe her current thinking. Just lay it all out, the story seems to implore. The main character lays the newspaper section down and starts to tell a story to the story about her great wish to help children tell the adults about their relationship with the natural world. The story has heard this all before and wonders which words would make the best nudge, sound least judgmental. The main character seems to speak with a new glint in her eye, a stronger resolve perhaps. The story is somewhat wary, yet hopeful. All of this tentativeness: just get on with it already. The story does not say this aloud, of course, too fragile the ego. The main charac-ter has meanwhile digressed from her plans to recount a dream that she had the night before. She was slightly younger in this dream and had gotten a job helping with swim lessons at an indoor pool. She arrived and tidied the area around the pool and met some of the families waiting for the lesson to begin. When an instructor failed to arrive at the start of the lesson time, she went to her supervisor, who looked rather haggard and uninspired. Her supervisor told her that she would need to teach the lesson. It appeared that the supervisor might have always had this in mind. There may have never been any certified instructor for the lesson. This is not clarified in the dream. The main character insists that she is a certified teacher and she knows how to swim, but she is not a certified swimming instructor. The supervisor essentially accuses her of a lack of imagination and bravery. Of course she can teach those children how to swim. The main character insists that parents will not be satisfied, will want to know that their children are being taught by a properly trained individual. To no avail. The main character returns to the pool, but much time has passed and only two irate mothers remain with their children. The main character explains the situation honestly to the parents, who maintain their fury, but not at her, and invite her to lunch. The main character feels that some dreams have significance in the waking world, and she wonders aloud to the story what that meaning may be in this instance. The story is perplexed. On the one hand, it would suggest that we are capable of anything we put our mind to. On the other, it would seem to side with the rising tide of credentialism and insist on a prescribed training to prove one's ability. The main character adds that after the swimming lesson, she led the children in preparing a fruit-filled salad of strawberries, raspberries, ground cherries, spinach, and some sort of dressing. This added detail helps the story to understand. The story announces to the main character that she is indeed supposed to teach these children something, but she must teach what she is led to teach, not what others wish her to teach. And the teaching is more of a facilitation than a step by step transmission of skills, unless that is what the learner requests. The main character is encouraged by the story's divination skills. The main character sits quietly for a moment and sips. The dream could also be an elaborate reminder to put ground cherries in the salad she is making for Thanksgiving. Outside the café, the winds are fierce. The oak leaves swirl. The main character observes a flock of seven blue birds. Another sign? From Walt Disney? The main character and the story look at each other and resume their reading of the *New York Times*. As the main character reads, her mind veers from the text in many directions, as it often does once she has consumed a strong cup of coffee. Just the night before, the main character watched an actress on PBS News Hour tell the world that her recently deceased father told her to always do what made her happy. The main character tries to remember any words of wisdom from her own long deceased father. He told her perhaps more than once never to stoop so low as to hate another person. She wonders now how he applied that in his own life, how often he might have needed to mutter those words to himself. She has long considered that he said these words in his own self-interest, in his effort to get her to speak to him honestly. They never really seemed like words to live by but rather words to remember him by once he was gone. Would her father have agreed with the father of the actress? Would he want her to do whatever made her happy? His actions would suggest that this notion served as his own personal mantra. His actions also suggest a corollary that the father of the actress probably implied: do what makes you happy as long as you do not hurt other people. The main character does not want to keep thinking about the wise words of her father. She recognizes that she might be on the cusp of some big personal revelation, but she feels that she has other fish to fry. Doing what makes you happy implies a kind of faith, simple or cosmic, that your actions will propel happiness will propel a sustenance which will nudge the motor forward. The main character feels that she has already pursued the things that make her happy but her main focus is the greater good, how to follow the path of greatest good with the time left. That path seems inherently happy and also maddeningly multitudinous. The stakes seem high now at this edge, this leap. Is that true or a figment? If change is incremental, can't the same be said for moving toward the greatest good? There are probably several philosophical treatises which could be consulted on this matter, certainly plenty of self-help guides. The main character glances up and around at the other customers in the café. Three young women and one young man sit alone at marble top tables with earphones in and laptops up, typing notes or drafts. One couple of middle-aged women sit in the cluster of low green armchairs and discuss some compelling topic with great animation. More ear budded young and middle-aged people stand in a steady line, together and alone, gazing blankly at the baked goods or out the window. The main character does not look directly in the eyes of any other person. The main character has the deer in the headlights feeling and gazes back at the text of the newspaper, considering individual letters and their serifs and the fonts alternating between headline and body. She thinks about the history of printing presses, the essential role of the Fourth Estate, and the demise of her daily newspaper of record in her hometown nearly a thousand miles away. She thinks about the privileged education she has received to be sitting in this coffee shop considering serifs and sans serifs, the education that gave her the meanings of these words and the broad knowledge of history that enriches her daily life. The main character is grateful and also impatient to see the wide sweep, the vast and deep meaning of it all. Trumpets, please. No, really, she does not need trumpets or clouds parting or golden light. A tiny mystical sign might prove useful, but she is not asking for favors. She did get that dream, after all. She suddenly remembers that she is sitting in this café with the story, and she looks across the table. The story is texting something with index finger and knitted brow. She tells the story that she would like to take a walk now, alone, and she will call the story later. The story nods absently and returns to tapping letters. The main character leaves some money on the table, grabs her coat, and enters into the swirling oak leaves, the fellow coats and scarves, the anonymous bustle. The main character thinks of a nearby favorite bookstore and decides to look for inspiration there in the tea leaves of the poetry section. She can also contemplate Christmas gifts on the way and once she arrives. She puts the deep thinking aside for now. She will plan to do that when she gets home, after she puts the laundry in the dryer. And calls the cable company, makes a salad, orders the yearbook, fills the birdfeeders, picks up the mail, and puts mint leaves in the dehydrator.

3

We write to document. This is why I write. This is why a blue jay or junco interrupts most manuscripts, incorporates. I heard that one woman chose to record television transmissions on four stations for twenty-four hours a day every day for thirty years. Part of me understands this need. The need to capture, not to honor or suspend, but to verify, note for those who cannot see, for those who come later, for those who do not know now that they care but who may someday.

Considerations that continue along these lines may then rely on the story to take up the slack. The story cushions the burden, allows the subject to change quietly, shifts everyone's gaze to the poodle or the ad on the television. The story changes the channel, turns off the lights, asks if anyone wants seconds. The story grabs the extra bag, holds the door, leaves the room to answer the door or the phone. The story takes just this moment to snap a picture or rearrange a shelf. We may all rely on the story without thinking about it, about the story or its parameters, its finite scope, its limitations. We may wish in this moment for a standing desk. Or wish to know how to carry on at a subsistence level, which sounds naïve. How to envision that edge in this space: gather the wood and acorns, walnuts and sunflower seeds, dry all the herbs, consult all the books in this house about uses for pine needles, learn to eat venison, learn to hunt and fish, save seeds, pull up the field for gardens.

4

This is a story of eyes and accretions, of identifying.
                                        of oak leaves, tenacious tannin
and mast. When all is said and done. Imagine that. This is a story of
failing to imagine that, of referencing instead the periphery, the light
peeking through under the door. This is a story afraid to imagine, truly,
abysmally afraid, a story that prefers to skirt. And this is the story of
triumph over that particular fear, a story of plummet, capture.

                                        Stories of weavers and slate
backed birds on gravel   Stories of those
upon whom nothing is lost.

                                The seeds and the seed
catalogs and the stories of the plants that will come in the springtime.

                                        Walk along river
banks,
                                        meander. Return
to the Cahaba and the Mississippi and the Choptank and the Susque-
hanna and the Hudson and the Thames and the Seine and the Tiber and
the Vltava and the Danube and the Orb and the Ohio and the Platte and
the Tombigbee and the Colorado and the Delaware and the Schuylkill.

5

The cast might include winter grass stems, eastern bluebirds, cooks waiting at the bus stop, postcards mailed to the White House, date stamps, de-accessioned library books, cedar waxwings, or pretzel makers.

The story of silence can be what you see vanishing but also what you imagine into being. Squint the eyes and gather the colors, form the fluency into a way home. Silhouettes of starlings, the susurrations versed into the open sky.

Wanted posters of harlequin ducks and chimney swifts. Wanted posters of shad and serviceberry. Wanted posters of longleaf pine and sassafras. Offer silent rewards.

Like the magic beans, but have we already buried them? Did the packets expire? Did we toss them to the wind already? Stir the leaves. Seeds will rest, may lie buried for decades. Under the right conditions of temperature, sunlight, and moisture, they will germinate.

Gather the fascicles of the eastern white pine, five fingers to greet you, and spread them beneath the hydrangea.

The grey squirrels may intervene; they often do. They may signal other intentions, new strategies for survival that we might employ. We may notice them more and more in the hopes of our shared survival.

Plant scarlet runner beans and magic tepees, lima beans and pole beans, beans climbing up corn stalks, soybeans that are not genetically engineered, beans to dry, beans to save, heritage beans, rare varieties of beans, multicolored and purple beans and black-eyed peas for the good luck that we will need.

6

When you stand at the edge of a deep valley, the slightest sounds take on a greater significance. They reverberate. If you instigate the sound, you cause the reverberation. The main character thinks again and again of the Rocky Mountains, a landscape she loves and barely knows.

She saw a pika briefly there and does not recall its voice, which she imagines has a high pitch, a squeak, like the sound of its name. She searches out the prairie dogs every visit along every roadside and is disturbed by the silence around them, the dim understanding and lack of care for their well-being, the deep mistrust of their intentions, and their entrenched branding as a nuisance. They whistle, unlike any noise of any east coast mammal.

The main character could list a hundred other species of interest, finds her curiosity at times crippling. The main character knows that many individuals dedicate their entire lives to the study and protection of an individual species or a family. Palm trees, armadillos, longleaf pine, koalas, diamondback terrapins, sandhill cranes, snowy owls, ants. The main character finds the idea of specialization quite compelling, but imagines that it would take her several more years to settle on a specialization, and there is not enough time for that. A happy generalist in capture and release of sound and sense.

                    to ask strangers
            this kind of data

                                    to be the scribe

            approaches a documentary truth

7

The main character
is
so many hundreds

8

The story maintains enough patience for the two of them and will continue to offer that gentle nudge and shoulder. The story could have left by now, but the story stays to remind the main character that nothing is too late.

The story sticks around to prod the main character closer and closer and finally beyond or over the edge. Erase the edge. Step off the rim. Jump

The main character hopes not to fray at the edges, lose track of the edges

The main character will continue to track the movements of the yard birds and birds in other frequently visited places, make notes, submit data.

The main character wishes to tinker more often with a variety of materials and little instruction.

A

meander does not end. It may inadvertently form an ox-bow, but it keeps moving

The fire

that is hanging over us. The climate indicators that suggest ramping up of temperatures higher and sooner than we had expected. This is a headline that the main character has not followed yet because she has been attending the bittersweet final performances of her daughter in the annual Christmas tradition of her dancing. The main character has not fully processed with the story what this edge means and how it felt to watch her daughter dance as a flower and a Snow Queen and Coffee for the last time, to know that this tradition has ended like so many other last times and traditions for this year, that one can think intellectually about the traditions that will come to replace them, but they will be the traditions of adult children who do not dance or behave as children.

The main character has always possessed the survival technique of shutting emotions into a compartment separate from whatever activity is in the foreground.

The main

character does not know if the emotions went into hiding with the increased questioning by others of the main character's emotional state. She does not know if the sadness did not appear because people were expecting it to, and this expectation shut it down. Perhaps the main character is simply stunned and awed at how beautiful her daughter was in the performance and remains as a human, and this propels her forward without sadness because the beauty was not lost with the ephemeral. The beauty remains.

Notes

This manuscript was written while my students wrote novels for National Novel Writing Month. I wrote 50 1,000-word blocks for my NaNoWriMo text and then erased most of the words. This was my plan at the outset, with the understanding that the narrative would emerge through the poems produced by this erasure, but another narrative grew as the draft progressed, or at least another way of telling the story grew, and I found myself preserving larger blocks of prose. The words are arranged where they fell on the page, and the titles for each section come from the text that was erased.

31   "Make our unknown known and keep the unknown always just beyond" was said more fully by Georgia O'Keefe in a letter to Sherwood Anderson, "Whether you succeed or not is irrelevant, there is no such thing. Making your unknown known is the important thing--and keeping the unknown always beyond you."

38   an imaginist: a word coined by Jane Austen in *Emma*: "How much more must an imaginist like herself be on fire with speculation and foresight!"

Acknowledgments

Thank you to my students who wrote captivating novels and long stories while I wrote the words in this text and to Barbara Hoekje, Carol Coffin, and Nicole Greaves, who carefully read through the iterations of this manuscript as I erased the words. Many thanks to Kristina Darling for her encouragement, to Elizabeth Savage, Marcella Durand and Lee Ann Brown for their insightful readings, to Aurelia and TT for their generous care, and to my family for their support.

PAIGE MENTON lives outside of Philadelphia where she runs a land restoration organization called Journeywork and cares for the land of a Quaker meeting. She grew up in Birmingham, Alabama. Her chapbook *Twenty Miles to April* was published in 2021 by Dancing Girl Press.

www.ingramcontent.com/pod-product-compliance
Lightning Source LLC
Chambersburg PA
CBHW031224120626
46545CB00003B/979